bumblebee dithyramb

joe rosenblatt

Dedicated to Faye and afanus bumblebees.

The song "Burdens" was composed by Faye Rosenblatt.

The author wishes to thank the Ontario Council of the Arts for a writing grant that made this book possible.

All graphics were drawn by the author and are reproduced here courtesy of David Mitchell and the Mitchell Gallery, 27 Prince Arthur, Toronto.

Some of these poems have been previously published by the Nation, Canadian Forum, Worker's Vanguard, CBC Anthology, Prism, the Ant's Forefoot, Ellipse 6 and in a book entitled Viva Che! published by E.P. Dutton and Co. Inc.

The type is 9pt. Century Medium excepting the titles which were handset in 14pt. Italian Oldstyle.   Printed offset on Multilith equipment at Press Porcépic, c/o General Delivery, 70 main Street, Erin, Ontario.

Mr. Rosenblatt is also the author of The LSD Leacock (Coach House) Winter of the Luna Moth (Anansi), and The Voyage of the Mood (Heinrich Heine Press). A selection of his drawings was recently published under the title Greenbaum (Coach House).

ISBN 0-88878-006-0

CONTENTS

THE UNCLE NATHAN POEMS

A HALL OF MIRRORS

I GET HIGH ON BUTTERFLIES

AFTERWARD

Burdens

With hel-i-copter power they bring their burdens home
some of them don't make it they fall in-to a stream and
drown their bur-dens bring them down
Bum-ble bees in black pi-lot caps a-
light on pastures of dreams

they drain the juice of the rose   they

drain   the juice of   the   rose

cool in the pond of flowers, while up a-bove some fly   with

hel-i-copter power   with sacks of gold dust on their

legs   their bur-dens bring them down

9

bees do gymnastics

Balloon Flowers

In the greenhouse
I'm staring down at pregnancies; tiny zeppelins-
skins: leopard
        clotted
                -soul's orgasm- bal
                        loon flowers

                        I reach out to touch
                        I tickle their ear lobes
                        rub the triggers
                        of each
                                balloon flower, they
                                don't complain, but
                                blush out
                                at my fingers, o
                                what distilled
                                manures & minerals
                                nourished
                                these
                                air
                                brothels.
                                I'm staring at bellies
                                clotted with leopard:
                                zeppelins swelling out
                                happy
                                pregnancies. ALIEN GLANDS,
                                they are not of this planet
                                these pregnancies: I touch
                                touch
                                fungus dreams, touch
                                passions of leopard
                                painted
                                on
                                blood
                                blood

                                blood

Who Painted The Crocuses?

Who, who painted the crocuses
painted the tattlers, the tongues
dipped in the duck yolk of orange:
these triggers invite
                 insect eyes
              moth in the onion's embassy
              tch tch tch
            ANTENNA trembles, touch. touch. touch.
terrestial ladies
snobs in mauve, yellow, & anemia
are, babblers begging
              immolation
              -the final solution to the crocus question-
is why the crocus, is more than a raving flower
but a follower, pushing filaments, ersatz pain
through the earth, as if to say
                      "HELLO, HELLO AGAIN
                        WE'RE THE DEBUTANTES
                        WHO SHARED THE HILL
                        WITH MISTER
                                  IMMACULATE"
but, who painted the crocuses?
painted the stem
social climbing
from Mother Nature's navel?   &
where did he sign his name
the painter: MICROCOSMOS MINISCULE
the virile stud, who
knocked all the crocuses up
family huddles, O my, how the crocuses look piqued today!
irritation, ULTRA FEMININES
menstruating anger, o what crocus lover
violate such midgets?
Not me!
for I'm only the phantom
who feels the crocuses up, & around
the shadow regions
with kid gloves, & love.
You see, a crocus gynaecologist
is not an easy job:
the hands in the cradle
they want to say
             "HEY SPORT!
             DO ME A FAVOUR
             WILL YOU POLLINATE MY NEIGHBOUR?"

& I want to say to them, the vulgar crocuses,
these birth bloomers!
                    "WHO DO YOU THINK I AM
                    . . . . A BUG?
                    DO YOU GIRLS REALIZE
                    THAT CROSS POLLINATION
                    INVOLVING A THIRD PARTY
                    IS AN OFFENCE
                              AGAINST
                                  MOTHER NATURE?
                    IT'S UNNATURAL
                                  INDECENT!"
Martyr flowers?
these are not Martyr flowers
                         but
                              bitches
                              punks
                              pushing up their short necks
                              above the ground
                              when the milks of winter
                                            melt
                              & the earth is a fire sale
                              alive, o alive
                                        with masochist tongues
                                        matchstick triggers
          then
              these crocuses are tourists
              visiting people, or
              the freshly painted house
              of Seymour, &, Alberta Levitan
                              in Vancouver.

The Bee is Breathing in the Womb

the bee is breathing in th' womb
the bee is breathing in th' womb
the bee is breathing in th' womb
the bee is breathing in th' womb
the bee is breathing in th' womb
the bee is breathing in th' womb
the bee is breathing in th' womb
the bee is breathing in th' womb
the bee is breathing in th' womb
      breathing
      breathing
      breathing
      breathe
      breathe
      breathe
      breathe
      breathe
      breath
      breath
      breath
      breath
      breath
      o, th' lovely bee
      is breathing
      in th' womb
      the ANIMAL
      is breathing

all th' wires of his leggs move
in th' breathing womb, hummmmmmm
th' bee is breathing in th' blossom
th' wires of his legs move
packing in th' pollen
packing in th' pollen
loco
motion
loco
motion
        back & forth
        back & forth
packing in th' pollen
in th' cavities
on th' rear legs
                back & forth
                back & forth
                brushing here
                brushing there
                look at the muscles
                on th' bee
                the bee is breathing in th' womb
                the bee is breathing in th' womb
                the bee is breathing
                in the urgent womb.

Jack in the Pulpit
is a flower with its fly open

Jack in the pulpit
is a flower
with its fly
open

Jack
is
a
GREEN monk
exposing
himself

Jack
is
a
religious
pervert
hooked on
chlorophyll

everything about Jack
in the centre
is true

he holds sermons
on sex education
in the schools

Jack in the sanctuary
with his pulpit open
is a lima bean
with gland trouble
in the house that Jack built
on Mother Nature's dowry

PURE Food

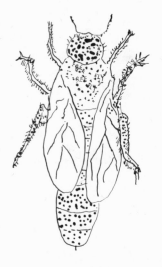

th' BEE HAS A BAKERY
  UNDER THE ARM·······
YELLOW BREAD···PURE
FOOD··· NATURE POWDER··.
th' BEE FOLLOWS th' DANCE
IN TO th' SHADOW of LIFE
EATS th' LOVE···
FROM th WOMB of DEATH___

Natural Prayer
(Poem for Several Voices)

ooooooooooooooooooooooooooooooooooooooooooooooooooooooooo, th' bees
bring home th' groceries, th' groceries, th' groceries, hummmmmmmmmmmmmmmmmm
                                                                          m
                                                                          m
                                                                          m
                                                                          m
                                                                          m
                                                                          m
                                                                          m
                                                                          m
                                                                          m
                                                                          m
                                                                          m
                                                                          m
                                                                          m
                                                                          m
                                                                          m
                                                                          m
                                                                          m
                                                                          m
                                                                          m

        mmmmmmmmmmmmmmmmmmmmmmmmmmmmmm
        o
        o
        o
        o
        o
        o
        o
        o
        o
        o, th' bees bring home th' dust
            th' bees bring home th' protein
                                        o
                                        o
                                        o
                                        o
                                        o
                                        o
        ooooooooooooooooooooooooooooo
        th' bees bring home th' powder
        plantation fields forever
        th' bees bring home magnolia bread
        th' bees bring home th' dust
        th' bees bring home th' bread, ooo
                                        o
                                        o
                                        o
        ooooooooooooooooooooooooooooooooooooooooooooooooo

20

I love to watch them pack, th' powder, in their baskets
I love to watch them pack, th' powder, in their baskets
I love to watch them pack, th' powder, in their baskets
                                        elbow baskets
                                        elbow baskets
                                            0
                                            0
                                            0
                                            0
0000000000000000000000000000000000
th' lovely bees bring home magnolia dust
th' lovely bees bring home th' bread, de,dum
                                       de,dum
                                       de,dum
                                       de,dum
                                           0
                                           0
                                           0
                 ooooooooooo
                 hummmmmm

Tribe Rhythm

tribal rhythm
tribal rhythm
     rhythm
     rhythm
     rhythm
     rhythm
     rhythm
     rhythm
     rhythm
     rhythm
     rhythm
     bee rhythm
     feet rhythm
     gland rhythm
     hand rhythm
     birth rhythm
     tongue rhythm
     sex rhythm
     body rhythm
     mouth rhythm
     song rhythm
     soul rhythm
     labor rhythm
     heart rhythm
     nerve rhythm
     blood rhythm
     psyche

rhythm
rhythm
rhythm
rhythm
rhythm
rhythm
rhythm
    dum
    dum
    dum
    dum
    dum
rhythm
rhythm
rhythm
rhythm
rhythm
rhythm
rhythm
rhythm
rhythm
    de dum
    de dum
    de dum
    de dum
    de dum
    rhythm
    rhythm
    rhythm
    rhythm,
    natural rhythm
    feet rhythm
    eye rhythm
    hand rhythm
    gland rhythm
    tribe rhythm rhythm rhythm rhythm

Animal Rhythm

ANIMAL RHYTHM
ANIMAL RHYTHM = TITLE
ANIMAL RHYTHM

ANIMAL RHYTHM, animal rhythm, animal rhythm, animal rhythm
ANIMAL RHYTHManimalrhythmanimalrhythmanimalrhythm,rhythm,rhythm,

rhythm,rhythm,,,

BEES DO, GYMN,astics
BEES DO, GYMN,astics
BEES DO, GYMN,astics
BEES DO, GYMN,astics
BEES DO, GYMN,astics
BEES DO; DO,DO,DO,
BEES , shave
BEES , shave
BEES , shave
BEES , SHAVE
BEES , SHAVE
BEES , SHAVE
BEES , SHAVE
BEES , SHAVE
BEES , SHAVE
BEES SHAVE WITH VACUUM CLEANERS
wwwwwwwwwwwwwwwwwwwwwwwwwwwwwwwwwwwwwwwwwwwwwwwwwwwwwwwwwwwwwwwwwwww
VVVVVVVVVVVVVVVVVVVVVVVVVVVVVVVVVVVVVVVVVVVVVVVVVVVVVVVVVVVVVV
BEES
        BEES
            BEES
                BEES
                    BEES
                    are POLLEN NIPPERS
                         POLLEN NIPPERS
                         POLLEN NIPPERS

                    BEES are animals
                    who return to the,
                              WOMB
                              WOMB
                              BEES, WOMB, BLOSSOM, BEES
                              WOMB, BLOSSOM, BEES, BLOSSOM
                              BEES, VACUUM CLEANERS, BEES
                              BLOSSOM, VACUUM CLEANERS, BEES
                              BLOSSOM, VACUUM CLEANERS, BEES
                              ANIMALS, BEES, RAPE BLOSSOMS
                              BEES FUCK
                              BEES FUCK
                              BEES FUCK
                              BEES FUCK
                                   FUCK
                                   FUCK
                                   FUCK
                              BEES DO, BUGGER BLOSSOMS   24

```
BEES DO,GYMNASTICS  , legs febrile
BEES DO,GYMNASTICS     hands febrile
BEES DO,GYMNASTICS      feet febrile
BEES DO,GYMNASTICS     tongues febrile
BEES DO,GYMNASTICS     eyelashes  febrile
BEES DO,GYMNASTICS
BEES DO,GYMNASTICS

                    POLLINATE, POLLINATE, POLLINATE, POLLINATE,
    POLLINATE pollinatepollinatepollinatepollinatepollinatepollinatepollinatepollinate
    pollinatepollinatepollinatepollinatepollinatepollinate  pollen
                                                            pollen
                                                            pollen
                                                            pollen
                                                            pollen,fly
                                                                    fallen
                                                            ,, fly
                                                             SUPER fly
                                                            fly
                                                               gland
                                                                    fly
                                                                        gland
                                                               gland
                                                                   gland
                                                             in football jersey
```

25

Bees are Flies with Gland Trouble

BEES ARE FLIES WITH,GLAND TROUBLE
BEES ARE FLIES WITH,GLAND TROUBLE
BEES ARE FLIES WITH,GLAND TROUBLE
BEES ARE FLIES WITH,GLAND TROUBLE
BEES ARE FLIES WITH,GLAND TROUBLE
BEES ARE ANIMALS
BEES ARE ANIMALS
BEES ARE ANIMALS
BEES ARE ANIMALS
BEES ARE ANIMALS
BEES ARE ANIMALS
BEES ARE, TROUBLE, in football jersies
                  , in football jersies
                  , in football jersies
                  , in football jersies
                  , in football jersies
                  , in football jersies
                  , in football jersies
                  , in football jersies
                   FLIES
                   FLIES
                   FOOTBALL FLIES
                   FOOTBALL FLIES
                   FOOTBALL FLIES
                   FOOTBALL FLIES
                   FOOTBALL FLIES
                   FOOTBALL
                   FOOTBALL
                   FOOTBALL
                   football
                   flies
                   flies, flies, flies, flies,

```
BEES ARE,FOOTBALLS,are vacuum cleaners
                     are vacuum cleaners
                     are vacuum cleaners
BEES ARE,FOOTBALL PILOTS
BEES ARE,FOOTBALL PILOTS
BEES ARE,FOOTBALL PILOTS
BEES ARE,FOOTBALL PILOTS
BEES ARE,FOOTflies
          FOOTflies
          FOOTflies
          BUZZZZZZZZZ
          BUZZZZZZZZ
          BUZZZZZZZ
          BUZZZZZZ
          BUZZZZZ
          BUZZZZ
          BUZZZ
          BUZZ
          BUZ
          Zz
```

The Spider

In his crocheted embassy
the spinning butler
entertains the lady flies -
monster of his operetta, he
feeds upon a half digested bumblebee.

The spinning butler
feels the guide wires of his planet -
vibrations will send him scampering
on eight allegro fingers:
mealtime is anytime - there's
no refrigerator in that sky.

David's Pleasure Dome

Thank you, David, your pet is neat -
under his plastic roof, his fishbowl palace
theologian of chlorophyl and claw
placed himself in position:
a dragonfly had climbed a wall
and the mantis who wore no sticky footwear
fell on his back, helpless as a turtle, a snapping turtle
and you pushed him back on his feet
with a long matchstick and resealed his pleasure dome.
The mantis trembled, serrated hands pinched the air
poised like a catcher waiting for the pitch
snapped him in his paws
the fly, the eyes black inkspots
diminished, wings dissolved like celluloid paddles in a furnace
there was a sawmill in the mantis mouth
Ringmaster, when's the next performance
when you offer him another live meal?

ANT god 'too much of' ON the RAMPAGE?

water mother

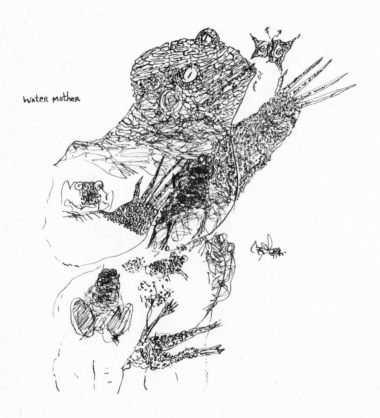

I Want to Hijack a Bumblebee

I want to hijack a bumblebee
& fly over th' marigold
home to where the fires begin

In the orange moonlight
I'll reset th' buzz machine's speedometer,
start from zero in th' centre
& when Death signals from his control tower
I'll take my flight out in the morning.

Poem for a Dying Bumblebee

The thorns know the hour
a dusty tourist strikes the rose -
flowers are not born; they grow
for this traveller in his tiny vestment
who falls on his pollen laden elbows
in Momma's tabernacle, in October.

Jesus Christ Dwells in Every Tulip

tulips
tu lips
are   middle class
    are status seekers

who desire to be stolen
from their beds &
moved to your living room
don't trust them
they are spies
they work for mother nature
tulips can be dangerous
tulips can be peeping vaginas

don't do it
don't.   leave them alone
        let them live out their lives
        let them identify with other tulips, don't!
& now they are focussed on you
MOTHER NATURE IS WATCHING YOU
she wants to know your taste
whether you copulate with indifference
whether you copulate with indifference
whether you copulate with indifference
whether you copulate
whether you copulate
whether you copulate
whether you copulate

        copulate
        copulate
        copulate
        copulate
        copulate

whether you eat   toast & marmalade
whether you eat   toast & marmalade
whether you eat   toast & marmalade
        toast &   copulate
        &   toast & copulate & toast & copulate & toast
        &   copulate & toast

tulips become upset
they can be jealous of your wife
they can be jealous of your sister
they can be jealous of your mother
they want to be more desirable
                    more sexy
                    more voluptulip
                    more toast & copulate
                    more
                    more
                    more

tulips have feelings
they dream sex
they dream toast & copulate
they dream of middle class homes in the suburbs
they dream
     dream
     dream
     dream   about getting laid by a bee
                  about friction
                  about having an orgasm
                  about fooling the bee
                  about jiggy jiggy
                  about bee's fur
                  about bee's stinger
                  about violence

tulips demand respect
they are super women
they are not inhibited about taking their clothes off
& tulips don't fight back

     they lie there
       restful
      & loving every moment of it &
         loving you &
                    toast & copulate &
                    JESUS CHRIST DWELLS IN EVERY TULIP
                    be kind to your tulip
                    your middle class tulip.

33

Mother Nature's Helpers

I
 love
      to
        watch them
                  violate
                        the
                          flowers

sometimes
          their diesel engines
          are shut off

          some of them
                    wear
                      black & yellow
                      swimming trunks

others
       are
          black hirsute
            & repulsive
                  virile
                    ANIMALS
                  with helicopter
                            powers

they
     weave
         in
          &
            out of
                  morning glories
                pause
                    in
                      neutral gear -
                      meditate
                    &
                      break into
                      a   kitchen
                      without a
                              search warrant.

WATER PART 2

The Trip

Please
Don't move my forest
the branches hide the children.
And a dog pawing open the grave
digs up my black attaché case—
late again at the office.
Goldfinch chokes behind the leaves,
a worm smiles. I've seen my death
on television.
It was very pleasant over beer—
I was a jellyfish puffing on a cigarette.

The boss in a silk tie came to dinner.
Or, to be precise, followed me
home. My fellow communards (commune living
is in this year) were offended
But,
I swear I was drunk
(my eyes were sore as editorials)
He was a boor and
I was weak. . .

There is a voice beyond the grave.
I lost my mind. The mortgage
of my reason was eaten by a worm,
was carried off by a bird,
to a high branch in my forest.
Help must be on the way. . .

Before I plunged like a fat robin
from the roof,
I saw a vision: I was a leftist Kubla Khan
pursued by mounted horsemen
from a belch of Mephisto fire.
Fellow commune members. . .
        you may hold these hands
        but place me gently on my cross.
        Be wise and catch my blood
        If you wish to invest in eternity.

As Mother Goose assembles her choir of birds
they fry my brains—
smell of ozone and furnace flower.
Don't, don't take away my forest!
Earthworms break the soil,
the mud of an ancient face
cracks, and the earth gives way
to stars below
Glow.
Dust.

From the eleventh floor
I search out that blond bitch (my wife).
The forest crowds her out.
But all will disappear
like a coded message
when they switch the channel on Saturday.
Their fog is best.

Toad Poem for John Newlove

The toad is down in the dumps
although he still enjoys humping
and phrenology -
it's his religion.
His mouth is parched.

In the hollow of a tree trunk
he dreams of straddlers on a lily pad
who'd take refuge in his image.
He holds back his song.

Sunday Toads

(for Bill Wilson)

In the daycare centre
they hop dots and dashes,
weigh every leap, fall
and blend in bark.
In this Sunday-School picnic
they count each other's bumps
have the comradeship of lepers
helping one another over their rough edges,
hating their sunlight health
and loving the poor acoustics where they hide.

Tiny Toad

Earth undertaker
eyes heavy lidded
has no song.
embalmed
in a tree trunk
five fingers say
out for lunch.

Song

Frogs have their own clan
in the tepid waters.
They sing a gutteral song
from a patio
& then do their dance
for when the marsh is silent
Life wears a serpent's face.

Virgil Visits Frog Hell

The plump paupers
in Death's nudist pond,
their skins oily
as though the great Bull Toad, Beelzebub,
had meant to give their skins to us. . .
belching endless methane,
they're cleft to rocks
until their shadows turn to granite:
would if they could
swim to the next lily pad
to Virgil standing there. . .master.

39

Toad 1

Cold bark, air...
jumping air
these tumors of mud
bumps on their flesh
worn like velvet -
field lumps that move,
leap
like frogs gone brown.

Toad 2

Earth
breaking away
from a
tree
trunk, leaping
into the shade
throat
palpitating
fingers outstretched
for
lunch
the plump camper
in the swamp
has no gleam
for a back-mate

Holy Fish at the Royal Ontario Museum

Compression of fish
sniffs out my cowardice.
In his belly
there is a sanitarium
of aphids.
They molested my mother's rubber plants.

On the Passover table
I drowned in the raisin wine.
The fish found my rotting soul.
There is calcium in his brown eyes.
He spews out the family upholstery
to get at those bones.
And the ghost will give him a pass key.

The Double Kingdom

Brittle sex
the coffin in flames
the machine reeling toward eternity
and the gloved hands tearing at the goggles
cremation thoughts
seconds away
from the blast
and the meat butterflies, the skull
in contact
with invisible energy
the skull
the pilot holding the porcelain vase
 pressing the bones and white tissues down
the mouth
anesthetized
for the perfect photograph
no more fish and chips
and a jolly good tea break
only the cold kipper kiss
at the other end of the universe
where celestial snails
are served on ice:
the final hors d'oeuvre
before the meat-self
is transformed
into thoughts
millions of vital thoughts
YARGGGGGGGGGGGGGGGGGGGGGGGGGGGH

the eyes move outside the skull
keep a stiff upper lip
it's only a superficial wound
says the mouth outside the face
can't be a defeatist ...
right, says the mouth outside the face
only a superficial wound.
The gloved hands push
the brain
back inside the skull.
outside the face
the lips stir.
outside the face
the blood
outside the face.
Death is just another trip
the blood
falls
outside the face.
Green Acres
just ahead, by God
there she is
the Double Kingdom
home at last ...
the pilot switches the engine off.

Extraterrestrial Bumblebee

i wish i were a bumblebee
i wish i were
an
extra
terrestrial
bumblebee
building flowers, or
locked in th' greenhouse
of my senses. . .
leaden eyes
heavy, heavy heavy heavy
o th' body sings
vvvvvvvvvvvvvvvvv
zzzzzzzzzzzzzzzz
th' soul weaves in, & out
th' soul weaves in, & out
th' bumblebee pays th' Passion Lily a visit
every moment is an afternoon
every moment is an afternoon
th' soul is in a full eclipse
th' soul is in a full eclipse, th' bumblebee is dark, is dark
o th' soul is in a full eclipse, th' bumblebee is dark, is dark
is dark, oooooooooooooooo
                              th' bumblebee is dark
                              th' bumblebee is dark
                              th' sun is melted in th' wings
                              th' bumblebee
                              th' sun is melted in th' wings
                              th' bumblebee
                              is dark, is dark, is dark, is dark
                              hummmmmmmmmmm
                              th' sun is in th' lunchpails
                              th' sun is in th' lunchpails
                              of th' bumblebee
                              of th' bumblebee
                              th' sun is in th' lunchpails, o
                              praise th' pollen
                              in th' lunchpails
                              of th' bumblebee
                              he grabs th' pollen of th' sun
                              th' sun is in th' lunchpails
                              praise th' pollen in th' lunchpails, vvvvv
                              th' lovely bumblebee, th' lovely bumblebee

shifts his gears, hums, & drives
in th' ocean highways of th' sun, th' breezes
th' breezes carry him
with his lunchpails
lift th' animal up
with lunchpails
into suburbia
th' animal hum
th' bumblebee hum
th' bumblebee hummmmmmm
th' bumblebee hum
th' bumblebee hum
th' bumblebee hum
hummmmmmmmmm
th' bumblebee wears a pilot helmet
his vision is blurred
th' pressure of compound eyes
th' pressure
26,000 eyes, 26,000 eyes
in each eyeball
his vision is blurred
hexagons, hexagons, o th' pressure, th' pressure
th' bumblebee, th' bumblebee drives
in th' ocean highways of th' sun
with his pollen lunchpails
& th' Passion Lilies cry out to him
'HURRY
          HURRY
          WE'RE CHOKING WITH POLLEN'

wet fingers hold th' pollen up to him
'O WE'RE SO DAMNED FERTILE', cry th' Passion Lilies
          'GET RID OF TH' LOADS,
          YOU DUMB BUZZ ANIMAL'

Bzzzzzzzzzzzzzzzzzzzzzzzzzzzzzzzz
sing th' bumblebee
     shifting his gears

```
                    moving forward
                          forward
                  over th' grieving
                          passion lilies
        fertile
                fertile
        knocked up
                passion lilies
th' bumblebee brushes away th' pollen
brushes away th' pollen
into th' lunchpails
   into th' lunchpails
                lunchpails
        into th' lunchpails
                religious
                golden
                pollen
                        th' Midas
                                bread
        O th' bumblebee's th' soul
        of a mole
        burrows into th' throat
        into Mother Nature's tenement
        & th' Passion Lilies cry
                'HE'S COME TO COLLECT
                TH' RENT'

th' animal is seduced
all that colour, all that texture
                        physical animal
                        taste th' Passion Lily
                        lick th' Passion Lily
                        draw th' tongue in
                        draw th' tongue out
                  & th' Passion Lily
                taste th' bumblebee
        draw th' tongues in
        draw th' tongues out
    taste, taste
    'here's th' fertile powder,' cry the white
                                flower
        'here's th' burden
         here's th' rent. . .'
```

the WATER MADAME

The Pilgrimage

The fertility pilot
flies into a cul de sac
of the soul

the powdered pilgrim plays
his rhythmic game
of Vatican roulette:
he impregnates
the woman in the flower

The Mushroom Factory

Mushrooms are elements of people
wearing turbans, they
puff out
like rubber moons: the bald crowd
on their love beds
incubate in the gloom
in the steaming horse manure & brewer's grain, pufff
I am being observed by fungus detectives
in foreskin raincoats.
Voices call out to me:
                'THROW US SOME SPORES
                YOU'LL BE A FATHER IN THREE DAYS'

It's an orgy, but no-one's touching.
The ghosts eat under their own canopies:
faceless gourmets
who believe God is an earth worm
living in the sterile subsoil
of perverted hothouses
where the dead reappear
in the land of tears.

Mother Nature's Proletarians

Bees are truck drivers of the sky
who burrow into diners of flowers
to be fed therein, & overhauled.
"I'll try another flower", think the honey bee,
"taste so goddam delicious, this flower
ummmmm...such O, dour, & colour".
Buzzzzzzzzzzzzzzzzzzzzzzz flip flip..
Pregnant with proletarian bug song
they carry their freight of pollen groceries
home to Momma—the boss queen!

Bees are truck drivers of the sky
who buzz into diners
demanding lobotomies for breakfast:
waitresses of flies scatter
before the maniacs of proletarians
—each blossom becomes a delicious body house
for diesel dancers in the atmosphere
                          Bzzzzzzzzzzzzzzzzzzzzzzzzzzzzzzzz
zzzzzzzzzzzzzzzzzzzzzzzzzzzzzzzzzzzzzzzzzzzzzzzzzzzzzzzzzzzzzzzzzzzzzzzzzzz
zzzzzzzzzz
        blip! blip! blip! blip! blip! blip! blip! blip!   zzzzzzzzzzzzzzzzzzz

    zzzzzzzzzzzzz ssssssssssssssssssssssssss zzzzzzz blipblipblip   zzzz
                                                                            z
                                                                            z
                                                                            z
bi zzzzzzzzzzzzzzzzzzzzzzzzzzzzzzzzzzzzzzzzzzzzzzzzzzzzzzzzzzzzzzzzzzzzzzzzzzzzzz
zzzzzzzzzzzzzzzzzzzzzzzzzzzzzzzzzzzzzzzzzzzzzzzzzzzzzzzzzzzzzzzzzzzzzzzzzzzzzzzzzz
bi zzzzzzzzzzzzzzzzzzzzzzzzzz   bizzzzzzzzzzzzzzzzzzzzzzzzzzzzzzz
buzzzzzzzzzzzzzzzzzzzzzzzz   zzzzzzzzzzz   zzzzzzzzzzzzzzzzz
bi zzzzzzz zzzzzzz   zzzzzzzz   zzzzzzz   zzzzzzzzzzzzzzz
z
z
z
z   z
z   z
z   z

z   z
zzzzzzzzzzzzzzzzzzzzzzzzzzzzzzzzzzzzzzzzzzzzzzzzzzzzzzzzzzzzzzzzzzzzzzzzzzzzzzzzz
                    Bizzzzzzzzzzzzzzzzzzzzzzzzzzzzzzzzz
                    z
                    z   z
                    z   z
                    z   z
                    z   z
                    b
                    z
                    z
                    z
                    z
                    z
                    b
                    e
                    z
                    z
                    z
                    z
                    z
                    z
                    z
                    z
                    z
                    z
                     z
                      z z
                     z z
                z
             z   z
               z   z
                 z   z
                   z   z
                     z   z
                       z   z
                            z   bees are, animal
                          z   bees are, animal
                         z   bees are, animal
                          z z   bees are, animal
                                                 bees are, animal
                                                 bees are, animal
                                                 bees are, animal
                                                 bees are, animal
                                                 bees are, animal
                                                 bees are, animal
                                                 bees are, animal
                                                 bees are, animal
                                                 bees are, animal
                                                 bees are, animal
                                                 bees are, animal
                                                 bees
                                                 bees
                                                 bees
                                                 bees
                                                 bees
                                                 bees
                                                 bees
                                                 bees

Cockroach Poem
- to commemorate the invoking of the War Measures Act in Canada

Make your peace with the cockroach
he's home grown, bilingual
was educated at Oxford, the Sorbonne . . . Yale . . .
- then of course, Goebbels -
roach in cap and gown
had a PhD.
The bug
found in the ulcerated stomach
of middle America
sings 'O Canada'
with passion . . . passion!
The skeletons of nine-to-five
cry for the whole loaf of political stability:
dissent is the rat's hair in the bread
and it won't be given the Good Housekeeping seal -
The liberals run before the suction cups of the roach
-"It's only a temporary measure"
The roach chews away
the finger of academia: the laughing grove
Or he takes his ablutions
in the dancing detergent
under the oval shadow of the hard hat
He's in the thick of maple syrup
and smells the sweeter for it
- like the deodorant of the living dead -
The erudite roach has covered every legal angle
he has eyes for incongruity -
every crack in the poverty closet has been covered -
The insect carries his retroactive retribution
to those fools who have attended meetings
that the roach has found unclean -
ah nostalgia . . . nostalgia
This larva has brought the vanguard of the super roach
small roaches at first
then commissar roaches . . . SS roaches
The legions moan in the darkness of the cupboard
The discontent has
by its 'dialectic' or natural carbuncle
of the class struggle
put the show on the road.

FROG KARATE

Action

```
comb dust
comb hair, dust
            hair
            dust
            comb
            hair
            dust
            comb
          basket
        dust
            comb
        hair dust
        gol,den
              dust
red, reed
          tongue
    draw
        juice
  legs
        comb back
            dust
      tongue
    red
        draw
        thin

        pro,tein
```

The Venus Flytrap

She aborted the first one
after her boy friend laid a fast foetus on her.
Retarded Lennie was a jerk working the steam pumps
at a caffeine sweat shop. He had a pair of horns for Gloria
wore a Stetson to hide the stems of love
while he pulled down the taps for cafe au lait-
& in that sauna of volcanic mist, he saw
-the jewel of his empire- Gloria
was vibing with a customer.

In the dark, Gloria pressured his palm
fingered a broken trench line.
The ghost giggled when she read out the message:
his departure due to strangulation, a lover's quarrel . . .
The albino's spoon sank under the marsh of coffee sludge.
He was 'cool' about the bad news
lit up a tangerined cigarette, halo'd a blue cancer ring
over to Gloria, followed by a squeak . . .
Mother did it
forced him to play a toddler's piano at four
slept with her baby 'til
he was fourteen, & funny.

The boy with the nervous coffee dew on his brow
raised his eyes above the machinery.
Poor Lennie, no self confidence, only guilt
& the urge to carry on the blood line.
He couldn't take his woman hotting to a pale hairdresser
with silicate painted finger nails pecking
a silver cigarette case, & smoking tangerined cigarettes
was most unnatural for the testicles
so Lennie animaled Gloria, rocked her little-man-in-rowboat
but good!

It was a dark summer for her delicate anemia.
Love had made an artichoke of Gloria:
her friend had lost his concrete shoes
& soon after left the earth's atmosphere
though everything seemed normal
but for the Venus flytraps making the scene
pushing out of the burial ground
taking a needled mouthful of flies, worms, & memoriums
& for a breath of air pollution
monarchs muttered into the air
molesting the sunflowers
that scattered their shitbrown seed
around the crematorium
while commuting tribes of lesbians:
bumblebees visited atrocities on the hollyhocks.
Collatorals of golden baby pablum
sneezed on thirty second notes . . . .
Mother Nature's vibrato-Gloria sighed,
the precious embryo was sleeping in her mouse church.
She said it was sliding . . . womb . . . sliding
said it as though that immaculate babe
could ooze out like a sea lion.

Gloria had less sense than a moth sleeping on a mothball.
She took a raincheck on suicide.
Doctor Magic cancelled her affliction on his lunch hour.
He would have given a mouse an abortion
for a bit of gold cheese.
The boy with the nervous coffee dew on his brow
grew a mean twitch over his right ear.
Lennie didn't fancy infanticide.
Mosquitoes of morality bit his nuts.
Gloria combed her blond stretch wig,
planted that cute ninty dollar fungus
over a blood clot on her scalp: the wig of shame!
thereafter, Gloria developed a phobia about meat
 believing in that timeless comic myth

of how the souls of funny people in shy butterfly disguises
take up their residence
in a breast of chicken.

A Letter from Marrakech

Human? the sub-midget
in a wheel barrow . . .
No arms or legs.
A robe covers what's left of him.
He is wheeled about the town by a smiling boy.
The tourists are entertained.
They whisk away the poverty flies
that crowd the glasses of mint tea.
FLIES. Great Jesus Mongolian Christ
I've never seen such affluent flies
not the housebroken variety: midget flies
but Moroccan hymenoptera
large as my finger nail
and they're laying bargain eggs for their Goliath posterity
on the lean chunks of meat on the shishkabab stands
laying marbles of death
excremental eggs
in the squat houses of their souls.
Every abomination has a soul
like the rats for instance
scampering across the park
I thought they were squirrels
They wheeze while they run among the orange trees.

Cripples, old men in their twenties
are muttering prayers or cursing me
because I'm healthy like those flies . . .
flies . . . flies sing their melodies
It'd be no use hitting them with DDT
They'd only drink it for their cocktails
and they'd grow fatter
in the garbage of natural selection.
The nasty bastards wave their coat tails up at me.
I can see their eyes gazing up at the sky.
They mean business, these unholy animals
nourished on shit, blood and mint tea.
I've seen them attack the eyes of blind beggars in the alley ways
and now they're buzzing their indigestion
in my mint tea!
I throw them bits of life preservers
and they alight on the bread crumbs
and pieces of mint . . .
flies who hate foreigners
knock against my glass
to get the waiter's attention.
The flies are thirsty
they're drinking the moisture in the air
They're subtly eating us
a piece at a time . . . eating, drinking, and crapping
but the sub-midget has no chance in his mobile domicile
who will give him a fly swatter?

A COSMOGRAPH

FROGS at their GAMES

Poem to a Flitter-Mouse

Flitting thru the blind
you, a metacarpis Christ
in rigor mortis awning
wiggle mouse tailed sword
to bounce sound
like a ghosting tennis ball.
Should I dispatch the ears
you'd be blind as a fossil
—a flitter-mouse in coal—

The White Lunch Cafe

Shadows with ptomaine faces
tribe in the White Lunch Cafe:
whores, pimps, mothers, snow birds,
cops and vanishing Indians.

Puffins of despair
so far down
that up is no higher
than murdered cultures
of spit & yesterday's
capsules & Panther Piss wine.

In the White Lunch Cafe
all meet in Fate's central urinal:
exiles fresh from the timber:
faces spotted with freshly filled graves.

The Dinner Guest
(THE MANDRILL)

The mendicant with greengrocer's thumbs
was ignorant of the water closet;
and preferred to foul his alfalfa nest
the dung was surreptitiously removed,
the linen changed. He was our guest-
the coprophile trumpeted a note
to bless the supper of his host
by commuting gas to virgin nostrils.

Fingers gesticulated. He made mystic signs,
scratched buttocks at the dinner table.
Tribes were travelling in his woolens:
drool slid from his lower lip
while he transfixed the wife with hazel eyes.
His design was plain as the stigmata on his nose.
He would need her cooperation
to fit him in her tiny purse house.

Saltpeter could not tame his appetite
I believe the animal was in love
for he had visions of her sanctuary -
and snapped his teeth for her photograph
cradling the soul print to his heaving chest
then, smacked his lips, & kissed her nakedness again,
belched a brontosaurus bullfrog, yawned
and love left its steaming dungball in the morning.

GROUP SEX —

Epilogue

THERE IS NOTHING MORE BEAUTIFUL THAN A BUMBLEBEE BRUSHING
THE POLLEN ON HIS BODY TOWARD THE CAVITY BASKETS ON HIS
REAR LEGS (HIS? I USE THE MASCULINE GENDER FOR THE BUMBLE-
BEE BECAUSE OF HIS NOISY APPETITE AND THE FORCE WHEREBY HE
BRINGS THE FLOWERS TO A CLIMAX. . .AND IN THIRTY SECONDS!
AND WITH WHAT ENERGY!) SCIENTIFICALLY, THE BEE (ANIMAL
ANIMAL ANIMAL), THE WORKER BEE, THE NINE TO FIVE BEE, IS A
STERILE FEMALE—CAN'T GIVE BIRTH TO OTHER LOVELY BEES. THE
BIG BITCH, THE SUPER AMAZON, THE QUEEN BEE DOES THE JOB.
THE CHILD OF MOTHER NATURE IS IMPREGNATED BY A DRONE (A
STUD WHO LOSES HIS STOMACH IN MID-AIR). THE BITCH FLIES BACK
TO THE HIVE. SHE IS TUCKED AWAY IN THE PRIVATE CHAMBER, FED
SOME ROYAL JELLY BY THE NURSERY BEES, THE HOME IS ESTAB-
LISHED. THE WORKERS FLY OUT TO BRING IN THE GROCERIES, THE
VITAL POWDER, THE POLLEN OF THE SUN. THE SCOUTS FLY OUT...
THEIR GLANDS ARE PROGRAMMED FOR THE JOB. FOOD, FOOD, CRY
THE GLANDS. ESSENTIAL, MUST FIND FOOD...POWDER, PROTEIN.
THE BUMBLEBEES ARE QUICKLY LOADED UP WITH POLLEN. THEIR
REAR SHOPPING LEGS BULGE WITH HEALTH FOOD. AND SOMETIMES
THE CREATURES ARE SO LOADED UP THAT THEY CAN BE FORCED
DOWN BY THEIR BURDEN AND PERHAPS DROWN IN A STREAM...
(UNLESS SOME LOVING PERSON COMES BY AND SCOOPS MOTHER
NATURE'S LOVER UP, THUS ALLOWING THE CREATURE TO CONTINUE
HIS MISSION, HIS GLORIOUS LABOUR: THE BUILDING OF FLOWERS).
BY RESCUING SUCH A TINY APOSTLE THAT PERSON WILL HAVE
TOUCHED THE MOST HYGENIC SPIRIT...PURE...PERFECT...AN ANIMAL
CLEANSED AND ILLUMINATED BY THE GERMICIDAL RAYS OF THE
SUN. THE BUMBLEBEE IS BLESSED, HOLY...AND THE GREEN LADY,
THE FIRST LADY OF THE UNIVERSE, MOTHER NATURE, WILL DELIGHT
IN NOT HAVING LOST HIM. HE IS MOTHER NATURE'S ASSISTANT, HER
PRECIOUS WORKER...EVEN LOVER! (HOW THE ANIMAL TITILLATES
HER MANY CLITORISES AND HOW SHE ENJOYS HIS WEIGHTLESS
HANDS, HIS CARESSES, HIS THREAD TONGUE). THE ANIMAL SHOVES

HIS BEING, HIS VITALITY, INTO THE ORIFICE OF THE FLOWER AND THE VAGINAL MUSCLES CONTRACT, HOLDING THE LOVELY BUMBLEBEE UNTIL THE ACT, THAT VERY HOLY ACT (PURE ODOR-LESS CARNALITY) IS OVER. THE FLOWER SIGHS, THE VIRILE BEE GOES TO ANOTHER FLOWER...THE BEE KNOWS THE WOMAN HE'S DEALING WITH, HER PSYCHOLOGY AND HER INTRICATE BIOLOGY. THE BEE KNOWS...HE ACTS (THE CYNIC WILL SAY: IT'S NOT REALLY SEX. THE BEES AREN'T REALLY MAKING IT SEXUALLY. IT'S SIMPLY THE PROCESS OF POLLINATION. THE BEES ARE PROGRAMMED). DOES IT REALLY MATTER? THE ANIMALS HAVE GIVEN ME INNUMERABLE EYE ORGASMS. I'VE TRIED TO IMITATE THEIR BIOLOGICAL SENSE DANCES...THE ELECTRIC MOMENTS...THE SUDDEN FORNICATIONS... THE OLFACTORY ATTACKS. I'VE DUG MY NOSE INTO THE WOMBS OF EASTER   LILIES. I'VE LICKED THEIR CLITORISES. I'VE INHALED THE SOPHISTICATED FRAGRANCES. I'VE TRIED TO LIVE OUTSIDE MY SKIN. I'VE BECOME NEUROTIC BECAUSE I COULD NOT CARRY THROUGH WITH MY CARNALITY: LAY THE FLOWER...I'VE BEGUN TO ENVY THE BUMBLEBEES. AND THERE HAVE BEEN MOMENTS WHEN I'VE BEEN TEMPTED TO SPANK THE BOTTOMS OF THOSE TINY BOOZERS DRUNK ON SHINE AND NECTAR. THEY CAN FLY IN AMONG EVERY SHADE OF FLOWER, PUSH OPEN THE JAWS OF SNAPDRAGONS, DRAW THEIR TONGUES OVER SUNFLOWERS. THEY CAN TAKE AN AFTER-NOON NAP IN A TULIP. MARVELLOUS, THE MUSCLES OF A BUMBLE-BEE...THE STRENGTH...THE CONVICTION, THEIR FULL EMPLOYMENT CARRIED TO THE BOUNDARY OF DEATH (THE FINAL ORGASM, THE DARK KINGDOM...FRAGRANT   GASES...LETHAL LOVE POLLUTION... AND THE ABSOLUTE SUN THAT WILL NEVER BURN OUT, NEVER...) THE BUMBLEBEE LOVES LIFE, THE SCENT OF CLOVER, A SEA OF PURPLE, THE NATURAL BODY ODOR OF THE EARTH WITHOUT CHEMICALS. IF WE COULD LIVE IN THE BODY OF THE BEE BUT FOR A MOMENT WHILE THE ACT OF LOVE WAS IN ITS STORM WE WOULD KNOW THE GREAT CLIMAX OF ETERNITY. THE TOUCH OF A BUMBLE-BEE'S FINGERS...THE RHYTHM...THE MUSIC...THE CONVERSATION IN THE FLOWER'S WOMB...THE THOUGHTS OF THE NEW GENERATION... THE ACT OF THE PUREST LABOUR...PERFECT UNION IS IN THE DANCE...THE STORM...IT WOULD BE A SEX TO END ALL OTHER SEX. OUR NERVES WOULD DANCE. THE BLOOD WOULD FLOW...

the
uncle nathan poems

I'm a silence so grim
no sparrow can flutter in
with its small music
nor can a child's innocent rhyme
catch me
where a wish grinds on bone
                Milton Acorn

Ichtycide

My uncle was Sabbatical crazed
wouldn't flick a switch on Saturday
but on the caudal fin of Friday evening
he'd be cutting up Neptune's nudist colony
into mean kingdom cutlets.
On Friday, Uncle Nathan lowered a butterfly net
to catch an Alcatraz shadow
dreaming myriads of muscled minnows:
spice cuisines of Esther Williams-fish pornography.

Lips ellipsing; a spiny Baptist lay on newspaper
blue leviathan with chopped up vertebrae
fanned fins in vendor's prayer
while scaly fingers mummified the prophet
-a fish head conjured Salome in a basket-

I too have knifed the sacred fish
have carnivored to please my palate:
a bass from a Chinese steam bath
lay in a puddle of Soya sauce.
This stranded swimmer on his oval casket
balanced death on optic centres;
animal penumbra expired for post mortem
I ghouled my way to the neck bone
then turned away from the Last Supper
for the eyes of Moby illuminated
or were they the fish eyes of Uncle Nathan?

Sleep Uncle Nathan, sexton in Narwhale's synagogue!

Uncle Nathan Speaking from Landlocked Green

Wide, wide are the margins of sleep
deep, deep, deep in the flowerbox earth
I sleep. .sleep. .sleep. .
In Carp's ethereal tabernacle
micron lips crackle
spirit embryos gestate
grow jinx wings, umbilical fins, slit gills
cold heart, lung, and lizard's spine
as from a cyanide back bone
flux of shadows strum. . .spiritons
from Death's encrusted harp.
Nephew, in this world
no dust remains, no nickle photos of our bones.
We are beyond dust
where spiritons and atoms hum
around a perfect planetary sun.
-such is spectral sex-
from worm to flourescent penetrant
in the grave, we all swing polar umbra.
Oye, so vengeful is Death's metamorphosis
that I go reincarnated in a minnow's whisper
who once dwelt as a barbaric fishmonger;
and now who can measure my sad physique?
                              Givalt!

or catch my whisper on a spectrograph.
Yet more soul pinching than worm's acetylene:
There is no commerce in the Netherworld.
Earth Momma, forgive me
for every fish I disembowelled was a child;
there is no Kaddish for aborted caviar.

Earth! Earth! is the bitch still green
liced with people and Aardvark powers?
And my shop on Baldwin street
does it stand?. .damp and sacred as the Wailing Wall
under the caterpillar'd canopy of God?
or has my neighbour swallowed up my Carp shrined enterprise
wherein I cradled images from Lake Genneserat
to fish fertiled ladies with halvah tongues
who shred my serpents into shrimp bread,
for fish food oscillates an old maid's chromosomes!
Carp, pickerel, transmogrified
where swimmers have been tranquilized
stomach's the body's palpitating madrigal.
God bless the primate's primeval stretch
but O to touch. . .touch. .
a moon's vibration of a silver dollar
to see the fish scales rise and fall
before Lent's locust of Friday's carnivores.
Nephew, heaven is on Earth; above me
the sky is smiling like a White fish.
Its eyes are the moon and the sun.

A Salmon Dying

This silver pickled salmon with gills lipping oxygen
he, Tarzan, pre-man, is caught in wash web.
                                          Cells break down
                                          sleep is a sun
                                          we orbit then.

"Only a salmon dying," Larry had said,
eyes gunning telegraph line.
Fish were biting. .concentrate. .concentrate. .
then, flapping my arms, I, Anubis, ran along the sand bar jackaling.

In the river, slapping, the salmon was dying
MASSIVE, even in death; domino black radar eyes zeroing zeroing.
Death was approaching. Approaching. I reached out. He was fog, and cold.

Across the river
                   tufted in parsely of lime green forest
                   the pulp mill closed its sexual energy
Dinner time: I waited for the fish to die, and the tide
                   like a cat's tongue, lapped water to sand
                   playing bird
                   with milk spittle. Fish mouth ballooned.
                   I paused. There was some resemblance. .UNCLE NATHAN?
                   Spirit, you ovulate more symbols than the Virgin Mary.

Water was cold. brrrr. .Christ was really a fish.
I imagined dying in a cocktail.
There are the finest nerves in an olive
And the eye
              being an eye
              can not see
                        computers.

In an olive
God's green voice is microscopic
as green is song
of growth.

                    vertical cells break down
                    we orbit then.

I saw the shrew of Death
enter the pink poem mouth
of the salmon tumbling, tumbling
                        salt drunk
                        with fingers
                        convulsing.

Concentrate. .concentrate. .close your eyes
sorry you're dying.
How many sardines do you archetype. .three?
Do you see twelve eggs on twelve supper plates?
In relationship to the sum of all conscious being

                    Who. are. you?

The Shell Game

Passing by the Jewish Funeral Home
(for I always set the time by the clock
in the living-room)
I suddenly encounter the orbs of Mr Z
the albino spectre
with a beard of laughing moonlight;
Z is emanating ectoplasm
a kind of chemical spirit heat.
Years ago Mr Z had fitted my uncle into a walnut;
I helped carry the shell to a midnight limousine.
The casket was weightless
or was Z playing a shell game on Sunday?
Now glaring at me through a window
more sinister than Kafka's cockroach
are the walnut eyes of Z.
In the darkness of Mr Z's palm
I lie quiet as a hopper
in a psychedelic match box
so peaceful
you can hear a fly sneeze
and then . . . a gust of warm air-
a voice squeezes through an eye dropper:
"For twelve hundred bucks
which shell is the poet under,
MR DEATH?"

the hall of mirrors

PART ONE

The Dance

I am in a hall of mirrors
inflections of light incurve
my image in ice

Icicles gleam out pantomime
I can not phantom the leading performer

                  myself
                  or the Icicle men

The object exists in the glass
I exist in the object
           I am
           a dance
           without motion

for the motion is with the mirrors
- the silicate kings -
who shallow the most splendid dance
by magnetic movements of their hands

Somewhere
in the dance
an octave traveller stirs

                  Arachne's fingers tremble
                  She spools out a web of glass
                  & the kings dance in the spider's web.

The object exists in the glass
I exist in the object
embodiment is motion

                  I am
                  a dance
                  or an image

                  I am
                  a multitude of dances
                  like a shabby moth
                  whose flight is caged in glass

The Dance Gells

Sky is pigment
In a cell
I am imprisoned

How do I escape?

all the fire exits are too small

wait!

I can ooze thru a pore . . . a door?

This is no Greenhouse

Glory O glory
I've found them
Two twigs of blood
lost in the ice forest
under a toadstool of snow

In the warmth of my hand
they dance for me
                    myself
                    & its shadow

but where shall we go?
back to Golgotha!
There's light in the forest

There's light in the forest.

PART TWO

O Exiled Anatomy

Across the wide plain
two glass horses sped
into a meniscus day
hooves of marble slit
arteries of earth freeing
exuberant geysers of fire
and myself in a burning carriage
was trapped in a bleeding heat
and thru my burning skull
horse and carriage raced
into the mirror of each brain cell

burning burning burning

                          the microscopic images in flame
                          the photostatic self in flame

O happy dust

               burning burning
                    mind
                       space
                             and organic matter
                  nucleus
                      and enclosing membrane

                             burning burning

O EXILED ANATOMY... EXODUS ... the self, somewhere
in the ultimate desert
where water is a myth
on the "Devil's Anvil"

and the reconstruction of those cells
is God

This world is an artificial flower
There is nothing real but the codeine and the wine and the codeine
and this deep drowsiness in the bud of the flower

I am in the bud of the flower
in the white stomach of the Sun-Dew

I slip quietly
thru a stem
into the roots ...

burning burning
burning

locust flesh

exhilarating ...

The Sun Dew

burning

O EXILED ANATOMY

PART THREE

The Seance with the Silicate Kings

i

I am stung by my own skin
by flat muted bees
in camouflage of pigment

automatically

        the kings touch the bud
        feel the depth of the bud
        — the violence of a sting —
        a red rose bud projecting.

Like a savory salamander
I live in fire
outside mythology

I am made of cellular vespiaries
neat nests are buried in my skin
Am I an intelligent protoplasm?
a social insect!
arachnid?

Define me then
YOU CANNIBAL KINGS

You have digested the Last Supper
the last morsel of protein
               my character

And now you have inherited the soul of a critic
                              a toad, a rat, a gnat
                              a louse, a house fly
                              a green parasite
                              a judge, a blood
                              sucker, a tape worm
                              and a
                                    snout beetle

Define me! you wizards of organology
                              I have two back legs
                              I have two spinnerettes
                              I have a thorax and
                              I live outside my skull

Is it any wonder I'm unhappy
                        and confused

              ii

The whirling boundaries of my dreams
are turning kaleidoscopic tables of the kings
where dreams change into ice blink patterns, or
you only dream you dream your dreams

And like a dragonfly locked
in the petals of my brain
my dreams are sweet and secret

O flowers of evening
buried in my skull
mandrakes
poison
thick roots of human shape
I know
I see
morose narcotic eyes
embedded in the faces of the kings.

YOU! Jacqueline YOU!
nude voluptuary swimming
in the blue meridians of my eyes
I close both lids . . .
but
    you
        quick
            like a slender jerboa
                    leap
                        into a landscape
                            of eyes

You will entertain the kings
be queen and bride of their fancy
attached like a precious butterfly
in the album of their hearts.

               iii

A swollen heart will need an umbrella
or a special poison
to numb a hornet of grief
but my eyes are fierce and flaming
like the battery eyes of a leopard moth

in lieu of love
I destroy all things
smaller than myself

YOU! mantis . . . green horse centurion
or priest with the big legs . . .
try and
        catch me
                try and
                        catch me . . .
            for the table is spinning
            and the kings work like feverish potters

Above an optic garden
a fly dizzying into space
I am
like the humming rhythm
of a deep deep prayer
a song gargantuan
with tiny wings

iv

the bud of the plant is sick but not dead
opens
     disclosing
          a tearful eye

        Jacqueline!

        indeed it is sad
        to find you in exile

but how is it outside this garden?
this optic miasma

we can not speak
we are
     like
         plants

we are hands, wings, stamens, or anthers of poison
we are not ourselves

        v

Life!
life!
   I say it!
   WHAT MADNESS

          I witness coercion
          an egg forced into larva and hibernation
          and wormed into a caterpillar fixation
          till it can't make its mind up
                  to be beautiful

          A Christmas butterfly
          or a happy
          wing slappy
              hawk moth.

Spirit!
      you can not engulf these sensous forms
      when death's gravitational pull
      keeps them in time with the cycle, the cycle
                            always the cycle.

          vi

The mute ventriloquist is brilliant
his minuets of fingers are spry movements of butterflies
a lyrical alphabet in flight

but who controls the ventriloquist
the alphabet, the strings of fantasy?
ah . . . the kings are clever in their disguises.

small hands stop vibrating
rest inward, find the silence
and form a prayer

the object exists . . .
I exist
      exist?
the strings are broken

The strings of the dance are broken.

I get high
on butterflies

Sun Poem

The sun
a peeping Tom
got his eyelids
thru the window
and brushed my desert brow.

I leaped
from the grave of a bed
and bolted the venetian blinds down
like a guillotine.
Part of his eyelids fell on the floor.
I'll sweep them up soon.

The World Egg
(an experiment in automatic writing)

I have dreamed this egg out of my mind, out of the picture, out of the
hatchery, out from the big end, that is, from a hen with big ideas; the hen that
has surrendered to sunlight, supervision, faith & intellect; and so I have
extended this egg, landscaped this oval dogma —the thing in itself— shaped
like a squint of God's eye; I have taken this egg from the reality of my pillow
and forced the egg outward and so, this egg is not a normal egg; an egg I
could hold in my hand; an egg I could

                                          tap!
                              tap! tap! tap! tap!
                                          gently

                              with a spoon; No!

          This egg is supreme
          this egg is the invention...
          the stuff of mental science;
          this egg is real
          this egg is ahead of Soviet science & U.S. agronomy
          & science fiction;
          this egg is the link in the space age & market research
                                          & laughing gas

          this egg will take a jet 10 years
                              to cross its dome perimeter.

I am walking on a blood speck, big as Lake Superior:
I am walking on top of the egg that will hatch another world, another God
                              another "ism", another anarchist,
                              another capitalist, another mother
                              another hen, another anything

     which means:
                    that I am walking on the dome
                              of the present & the future

          that I can look out and see death flying
                              like a bat
                                   or hen;

92

        flying against the mouse of mankind

which means:
        the egg, the egg poem

can never be finished

the metaphor has been crushed by the egg...miles of egg spanning
                       into time & beyond time,
                       out out out
                       beyond even the element
                       and the egg keeps growing
                                bigger & bigger.

I have dreamed this egg out of my mind, out of the picture, out of the hatchery,
out! out! way out, and so I have extended this egg, this oval dogma, this bird
tabu, this whole egg —the thing in itself—; I have landscaped it out over the
world, for the multitude, to see the egg, to gaze with wonder, to ponder &
pray to the egg; I have taken this egg from the reality of my pillow and forced
it outward, so this egg, this very logical egg, is not a normal egg, an egg I
could hold in my hand, like a golf ball; No! .. it is not a normal healthy egg you
could find on your shelf in your home;
        it is not an egg I could tap!
                                        tap! tap! tap!
                                           gently
                                      with a spoon

            I need a steam shovel
            to tap this egg

            I need an ocean
            to cook this egg

            NO!

            this egg is supreme
            this egg is the invention.. the stuff of mental science..
            this egg is not a dream
                        the dream is in the world egg

            the dream is lost in the world egg.

'He's after MY BODY'

The Easter Egg I Got for Passover

The body of Christ did not go to heaven, the moderator of the United Church of Canada said yesterday. Right Rev. Ernest Marshall Howse told a press conference that he does not believe in the physical resurrection of Jesus, but does believe in a spiritual resurrection.......... —Toronto Globe & Mail. April 23, 1965

....so much pain around the Easter egg, the Easter egg! the Easter egg! with paschal scenes around the Easter egg; spikes, lilies & fallen angels inscribed, in Persian space around the Easter egg; and the ladder, the safety ladder, miraculously, held up by air (painted blue). And now this figure dressed in a cloud suit climbs out of the ground looking as though he'd slept there for several days on a uranium mattress, because he's all radiant, even his gown, which is spotless. He climbs the safety ladder, the ladder that keeps leaning against the sky. He climbs the ladder, sleepy, tired, maybe he's been on dex- idrine, because he's haggard, bent over, like some of those freaks I've seen around the Village, walking the expresso mile. The bearded man keeps scaling the ladder with a most violent headache; burning disc orbiting like a hummingbird around his skull. Still haggard and bent, he progresses up the ladder, now and then assisted by two sexless angels who act as his bufferin. He stumbles up the ladder, the clouds are directly ahead (painted white); below, at the base of the ladder, a pastoral mob, shepherds & lambs & albino doves are sprinkled in the area. Now the audience is awed, stoned by this whole business. Imagine! a man climbing to heaven, without even a para- chute! Good-bye! We'll miss you on earth. Yes, send us a thunderbolt when you've made it. And the air keeps holding up the ladder. There's something wrong with this egg I got for Passover. I'm going to send it back, but there's no return address on the egg, the egg I got for Passover, the egg with so much pain painted around its belly. I'm going to knock on the egg. I'm going to find out who has sent me this egg...Knock! .. Knock! ..No answer.. Knock! Knock! No answer? Knock! Knock! Knock! .. No answer, but a hand reaches through a crevice, and the hand drags the ladder through the crevice.

It's in the Egg
IN THE LITTLE ROUND EGG

We are continually bored with the air,
the round doors, the flat tables, the straight spoons,
the whole damned breakfast ritual, the toast floating in the air
and suspended above our heads and the egg, the little round egg,
the paranoid egg, laid by the round hen in isolation;
the egg, the hen, fertilized by unnatural forces,
the light, the ultra blue light working
first on the bird and
then the egg, the little round egg balanced
on its little bottom
on our square plates.
and now the impression of tiny fingers working
at the top or the bottom
of the egg, always the round egg—
and our fingers, our precise fingers
digging, probing the round egg
like a conspiracy
like the egg contained the secret of the Sunday bomb.
it's in the egg
in the yolk of the egg;
the little plans
the final solution for the human race
it's in the
yolk.

And now I can see it
the blue light working on us,
urging us to tell everything,
all our intimate living,
the colour of our bank accounts;
details, details, details,
it's in
the
yolk.

And now all our fingers work furiously,
all six tiny fingers probing, digging
deeper, deeper,
into the guts of the egg.
it's in the egg in the yolk of the egg in the yolk
of the egg in the yolk of the egg in the yolk —
of the little round egg.

We are continually bored with the air, the round doors, the flat tables, the
straight spoons, the whole damned breakfast ritual, the toast floating in the
air and suspended above our heads, the golden brown toast, the delirious sunny
toast, the toast begging to be anointed with margarine, the toast dipped in
the yolk of the egg, in the yolk that tells all.

The Electric Rose

"Get out of the way," she whispered,
"you're stealing my sunshine . . . my photons"
An optical illusion, I concluded
as the obscene lips of the rose
closed.
I watched the rose glow;
her body was a crucible of fire
and her stamens . . . electrodes!
The redolence of the bud
held me in a trance
till a rustle at my feet
drew my eyes to some weeds
sneaking up like green landlords.
"Save me!" cried the rose,
"They've been after me for weeks."
"Okay lady, what's your name?"
"PHOTOSYNTHESIS," said the rose.
"Go on ... you're putting me on," I replied.
"Hurry ... PLEASE ... " cried the rose,
"They've been tickling my root hair!"
I reached for her throat.
"Get the roots ... the roots ... you silly rose beetle!"
Burrowing my fingers into the ground
I found the root
along with a broken finger nail.
"Easy ... pull ... gently," said the rose.
As I pulled her from out of the ground
a mob gathered around my feet;
"Give us the rose," demanded the stranglers.
The verdant Mafia in their yellow sombreros
were crying for blood
but I would not appease the dandelions.
The rose collapsed in my hand
mob-shocked and pale.
I carried her up to my room
where I mended the broken root
with iodine and bandaids.
In gratitude, the rose electric
beamed like a Bessemer converter
and recited a poem
from Li Po.

SWAMP
OGRE

The Bee Hive
(AN ELEGY FOR CHE GUEVARA)

I don't believe in ghosts
yet surgeons transplant a living heart
into the chest cavity of a dead man
a pulping orange
. . . . . . .a new ticker!

But for a bullet hole in the heart
there is no second valentine for a Marxist.
The worms have murdered the tiger. Che is dead.
And in time, we too shall face the bee keeper
for they who move with tender feet
thru the saw-mills of the hive
they shall hear a hymn of Carpenter bees
whose furnace song is dum-dum's liturgy.

In secret ground they've buried Che's dust
trembling like monks who hide religious radium
from the lead eyes of the poor.

Egg Sonata

I

"The Chick Peepeth From The Egg"

—Akhnaton

To an ounce and a half of energy strutting around in the palm of my hand
I say: congratulations...,you've made it;

don't blame you for being mad at me,
digging your beak into my finger,

don't blame you for looking up at me with defiance
like I was responsible for you being in the egg in the first place;
congratulations! you've made it, nosed your way out of the egg;
a poet would have died there, deciding he was mad, curled up and died there
in a perfect oval nightmare, but you my little refugee, are here in my palm
scratching for the answer—your have an Oedipus fixation,
you think I'm responsible
for your situation, and bent on revenge, you follow the life line in my palm—

would I have made it in your place?
don't really know;
it's tough on your nose
breaking the enamelware

then suppose, your nose is kind of soft
what then?
it makes me sweat!

O birdie! congratulations, a thousand times congratulations,
congratulations! congratulations! congratulations!

Yes! every morning at breakfast I get kind of religious

how fortunate I am
breaking the egg
from the outside
instead
of inside
out.

II

Let the egg live,let it be lowered,into a flower pot and buried in loam,and yes,
let the egg dream in technicolor, dream black loam and sunlight, egg-plants,
pear shaped purple enigmas, fruition—
                    the last vegetable fantasy of the egg and not Canadiana
                              —a dull maple leaf—

the egg should live forever, the yellow yolk endeared to the egg, loved
                                        by the oval exterior
                                        slick art form
                                            erotic spheroid!

this morning I've cooked
                    —a wild enormous egg—
                        intact on a plate
                              I've scalped a hole
                                        in the plaster

the spoon gouging out
                the egg, gouging! gouging!
                                        for dead
                                        dinosaurs, crocodiles, lizards
turtles, kingfishers, albatross, webbed toads, flying dragons, salamanders,
golden eagles, herring gulls, blue jays, great horned owls, peregrine hawks,
Canadian mallards, deadly hummingbirds, garden snakes, seedy romantic
poets...

                              what evil lies in the egg?

III

"Mass production methods sweeping the egg industry have given Canadians
the lowest egg prices in more than 20 years..."
—Toronto Globe & Mail March 5, 1965

EGG PRODUCTION CRACKS PRICES
or
Depression Time For Hens

the price of eggs is falling—
thirty-five cents a dozen
that's three cents an egg,
that's depression
        for the farmer
        the hen
        and the egg, unwanted,
        unloved;
                —a sphere of melancholia—
             on our breakfast table.

        the egg
                can't hide its curved feelings,
      enamelled skies crack,
                      the egg, emotional...
                      shell-shocked and broken...
                      spills its yolk heart
                      out on the breakfast plate.

It's a bad year
for the farmer, the egg, and the hen
                that's depression
                that's automation
                that's exploitation

        the perfect Canadian hen, reduced
        to a second class bird, a bum,
        a prairie chicken, a tramp,

                pimped away on the market
                for practically nothing...

        soon the eggs will roll out of gum machines.

Waiter! ...There's an Alligator in my Coffee

Waiter!...there's an alligator in my coffee.
Are you trying to be funny?
he said:
what do you want for a dime...?
...a circus?
but sir! I said,
he's swimming
around
and around
in my coffee
and he might -
jump out on the table...
Feed him a lump of sugar! he snarled -
no!... make it two;
it'll weigh him down
and he'll drown.
I dropped two blocks of sugar
into the swamp
two grist jaws snapped them up
and the critter -
he never drowned.
Waiter!...there's an alligator in my coffee.
Kill him! Kill him!
he said:
BASH HIS BRAINS OUT
WITH YOUR SPOON..!
By this time
considerable attention had been drawn:
around my coffee
the waiters, the owner,
and customers gathered.
What seems to be the trouble?
the owner inquired,
and I replied:
There's an alligator in my coffee!
...But the coffee's fresh, he said
and raised the cup up to his nose...
Careful! I said,
he'll bite it
off
and he replied:
How absurd,
and lowered the cup
level to his mouth and
swallowed
the evidence.

Paddy Stanton

That awesome power plant
deep in his chest failed
when death the mad mechanic
on the morning shift
scabbed the operation.
He died in the morning
in the harness of the class
of which he was so proud
to be a member.

A GIANT
he shaped an earthy language
into a spear,
so every "pie card"
climbing his Jacob's ladder
to a palatial office
knew their epitaph was his name.

In the summer of '33 they followed
a prairie star to Regina
and a boistrous convention resolved
a quick funeral for capitalism.

The years passed:
the undertaker becomes a caretaker
and in a rabid blistering hatred
they banish him from the party
for challenging a pale encyclic.

Their brutal kinsmen
in the Iron Workers Union
muzzle his voice
with an edict:
pay your dues — keep your mouth shut!

A cerebral monitor flashed
to a few of the time-servers
who pushed aside their sirloin-
plated expense accounts
but perished from an inedible mushroom
of a marriage with their past.

The others drift into old age
in the parliamentary gas house
before the real issues
come to the top of the order paper.

I once gazed into the maw of a river
roaring in perpetual anger
and saw the portent of a new Spring
when the globe trembles
and the giants span the continents.

I Get High on Butterflies

I get high on butterflies;
the way they loom in the air
and land on air-dromes
                    of petals

and with nervous wings
shake off their colours
                    of orange, green and blue...

I get high on butterflies;
their very names:
                    Tiger swallow tail
                    Zebra
                    Pygmy blue
                    Arctic skipper
                    Spring azure
                    Common wood nymph.

Caught in the net of my mind
they whirl around
                    and around...

The Lovers

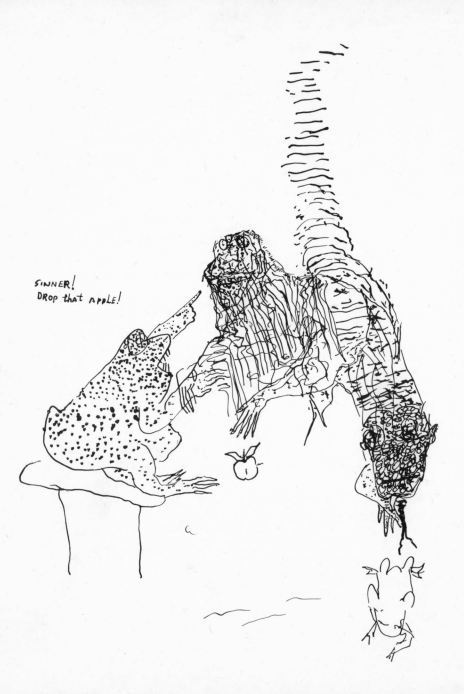

Jealousy

There is an orang-utan inside of me
and he jumps excitedly
when you throw your piranha eye
at me with scorpion's affection.
Take me apart,
one onion skin at a time,
only please don't
whittle me away with your eye
as you would
a hunk of wood.

Grass Head
(THE HEMP SMOKER)

You have watched the table legs grow in the room
and your eyes are heavy with sleep and o,O!
how your head is stuffed
with sweet grass and nicotine.

you sit on a chair
you're not certain
the chair is a chair

the chair has four legs
you have two legs

you could be a chair,
you have two arms,
that would make four legs

you could be
a chair,
a table,
even a bed,
you could be important

11

There is a worm dancing...
in your humpty dumpty
head;
a kind of tobacco worm,
green and fierce
thinks your brain is a leaf
                    -of happiness-
                    stupid worm!
outside your head -
nothing exists,
except -
an egg
boiling
in a pot of water.
the egg is white
it has no expression

you touch your face...
with the hands...
of a chair,
with the hands...
of a table,
with the hands..
of a bed

you touch your face
you believe
your head is in the water;
the outline of your face
is
like an egg

-suddenly!-
you're frightened, -
of the egg;
the egg,
that has no expression -
the egg, the pale
unhappy
egg.

the worm gazes thru your eyes;
he can see that you're unhappy
and he is bored,
and dances in your head.

111

It seems that egg has taken hours to boil;
there's something tragic about an egg
that won't boil;
a minute is a centipede a minute is a centipede
                              a minute is a centipede
it has one hundred legs

WHY DOESN'T THAT EGG BOIL?

it doesn't matter, it doesn't matter,
that the egg won't boil in this century.
a minute is a centipede a minute is a centipede
                              a minute is a centipede
it has one hundred legs.

The House Painter

The thin blood filament streaking
across the corner of his eye
is a truth I squeeze out of my mind
like a sponge.
And the colour of health gone
from his iron laced face
is the judgement of paint and turpentine.
Once when jobs were scarcer than four leaf clovers
he gave me pocket money for a year
so I could afford pride.
And when curiosity bugged me
to open the family chest,
I found a poor people's hospital card
among yellow soiled family photos.

Love

A wee Koala bear
climbs soft branches
of your fingers,
rubs his worldly nose
into the palm's eucalyptus.
Like a wild wallaby,
a loose-skinned tangerine,
the heart leaps out.

The Work Shift

I gather my crooked work boots
that Christ should have worn
along the road to Golgotha
and the boots have a certain personality,
they're starved from a lack of polish and
broken through from labour, eaten by the very
life's dust, just like some people I know.
I place my warped feet inside the crooked boots.

Every afternoon (except Sat. and Sun.)
the round face of the 'Silver Bell' alarm clock
shrieks out a prolonged shrill dagger
that mutilates the egg shell world of my dream.
O how I love to sleep, I'm obsessed by sleep,
because I'm tired like those boots.
About 2:30 p.m. I'm out on the street, dragging
my clod-hoppers along the pavement and
I'm aware of the sparrows digging me over
with their J. Edgaring eyes:
at the corner of Avenue Road and Davenport,
the cops are loitering by the bank
like scarabs around a dung heap.

3:00 p.m. I'm at work unloading a C.P. Express trailer
and a wired box prison of miniature ground hogs
-guinea pigs marked up for the cancer factory-
moves along the belt:
so I think the only difference
between me and that family
is that I take a longer road to hell.

A God of his pond
Bullfrog is glum—
& swells into a tyrant
a patriarch w. the swamp—
His harem is baptized
His children — water patriots—
ELEMENTS of ALLIGATOR DISSOLVE—
THE FUTURE is a FLY in his mouth
THE AIR is thick with PRAYERS
THE water is stomach & NURSERY
The Boss. is GLAD at times
HIS EMPIRE GROWS AROUND his MIDDLE

The Black Flower

It is a black flower
a flower without fragrance
detached like Death -
that small limbed girl
with silver hair
who in cosmetic consciousness resides -
narcist limbed in a glacial world.

I extend perception, perceive
aesthetic organism spinning
geodesic lines - filaments of love -
until, caught in a swoon of sensitive labour,
the spider lies exhausted on its back
and changes to that special flower
with eight tall stamen legs.

The Herd

I see more love in iodine bottles
than in those faces passing before my eyes
like lantern slides; faces so frozen
that even the concrete seems more alive.
I see them pouring out on the pavement:
a deluge of ants
from out of some dry dead wood.
Urgent legs move like fingers spidering
the nerves of a guitar;
so that I become radioactive watching
the rhythm, the flux of bipeds.

Outside my seperate cocoon
the robots, the multitude, gather at the zoo;
at the mirrors of their province
to goggle at the Sunday apes
who pick their narcissistic noses
like human kind and love it.
O, how blessed...these apes
bugged by attitudes of voyeurs.
What hipsters!...those families
caged like people in their living rooms
and the apes have nothing better to do
than watch the herd.
Ah...such oppressive boredom!
I see more love in iodine bottles
than in those faces passing before my eyes.

I Was Afraid of the Sun

The sky was the colour of azure
It was the natural effluvium
of millions of Azure butterflies.
I was afraid of the sun
I suspected of being God's monocle
blazing to burn me alive.
It was only a suspicion, spun
in my fine theoretical brain.

The sweet songs of the morning
filled me with nausea:
I hated the song sparrows lurking
in the ugly yard,
these small musicians daring to give me
their looks of pure innocence.
Only the green mantis I loved
with its long sexual legs
bent in meditation (to the east)
I loved its sincerity.
O tiger of the insect world
how I wept, when in a moment of love
the female mantis devoured you.

I was bored.
I counted the seconds
that made up my paradoxical day
when a fleck of night
danced by my casket.
It was a black Swallowtail,
It was bad luck
and I chased it away
with the help of a friend,
a white Luna moth.
We fled together, the moth and I
into the quicksand of darkness.
I was afraid of the sun.

The Funeral of the Great Bull Frog

Pater Noster went damp with tears
with the last croak of the bull frog.
He was quite dead when they found him
on a lily pad.
The procession included:
four lizards
a chameleon who wept brilliant colours
and a horned toad who led the ceremony.
They buried him
at the bottom of a pond.
After the funeral
the friends of the deceased
held a feast of pygmy blue butterflies
which induced a forgetfulness.

Metamorpho 1

        Lately I've become religious about atoms
and this is how I've come to dig the element man,
Metamorpho, freak with a 103 personalities

                -the do-it-yourself chemistry set-
like
   ...''don't get tough with me baby..or I'll explode!''
grrrrr...I'm hydrogen
           I'm hydrofluoric acid...hssssss..
I make pretty bubbles...I react with zinc
              I'm a real base character
but Christ, NO! I am not Prince Metamorpho, nor was meant to be,
ugly and priceless, working myself into an atomic warhead,
a gold brick, a platinum egg... priceless..

poets give off so much laughing gas, but not Metamorpho
who comes on in metal metaphors: aluminum, copper and cobalt;
chases his tail with a tungsten tool, losing atomic weight
and burning up like phosphorus
              before he flips his molecules
              into an osmium
                  omelette

Saphire
(METAMORPHO'S CHICK)

Saphire, you throw more curves
than serpents in a serpentarium;
you slide your sex
          like a snake
from Medusa township
          as you curl the question: matrimony,
before the ugly American ...Metamorpho!
but he won't marry you
          not in his crazy chemical state...
who could love that titanium face?
not his mother, that's for sure!
why he'd scare a grasshopper.
Lay off this element boy, this chemical creep,
think of the children, the ostracism..
you're going to get burnt
he's going to turn into a Lucifer
and burn your lovely ass
          watch out baby
          don't push him too hard.
leave the freak alone
leave that gun zippered in his holster
don't play gang busters below the hips,
instead, play with your daddy's Japanese toys
          and not with the voltage.
what perversity!
          copulating with carbon dioxide
you're sick, my little flower, sick
but he's odourless
as he changes from a gas to a sickly skull again
it's enough to make an iodine bottle throw up
          its bones
He ain't human baby and that's a fact!

The Bullet Proof Jew
for Al Purdy

I've been absorbing the luminations of Metamorpho
there's tears running through my fingers
so everything I touch turns lachrymose;
the hand of pathos grips me from a comic strip
where God in Metamorpho dwells in technicolor;
Dear reader: there's wonderous sublimation
beyond your scope of comprehension
as Metamorpho changes to a body of hydrogen
but I mere mortal can not float
with Metamorpho into the atmosphere,
escape the ennui on earth.
If I could rise like a spirit from a shawl
I'd trade my original Capt. Marvel comic book
to be that floating Jew in the ionosphere
                                        and bullet proof.

AN INTRODUCTION AFTER

by bpNichol

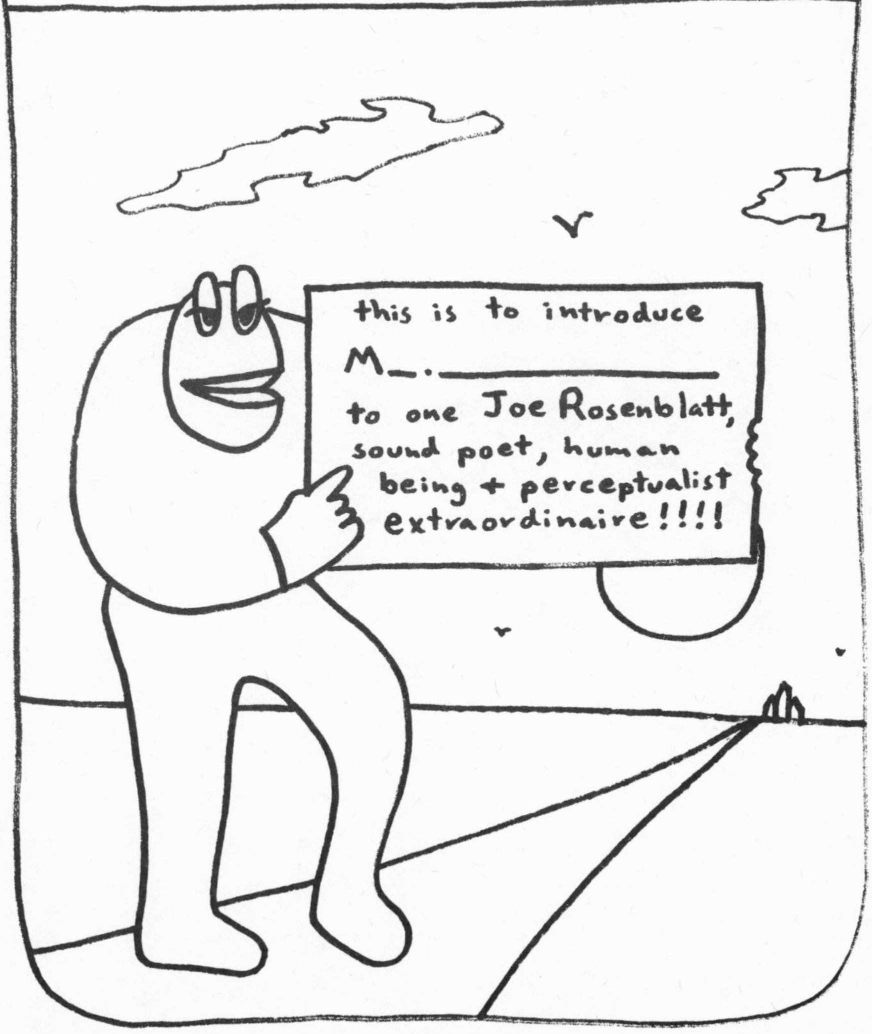